Little
Hawaiian
Mango & Papaya
Cookbook

Little
Hawaiian
Mango & Papaya
Cookbook

Compiled by Joanne Fujita

MUTUAL PUBLISHING

ISBN 1-56647-729-8
Library of Congress Catalog Card Number: 2005927294

Photographs on pages 1, 3, 12, 20, 27, 28, 34, 38, 41, 49, 54, 56, 65,
and the cover by Ray Wong
Photographs on pages 5, 7, 17, 43, 47, 50, 58, 62, 71, 72, 74
by © Douglas Peebles

Design by Sachi Kuwahara Goodwin

First Printing, July 2005
1 2 3 4 5 6 7 8 9

Mutual Publishing, LLC
1215 Center Street, Suite 210
Honolulu, Hawai'i 96816
Ph: 808-732-1709 / Fax: 808-734-4094
E-mail: mutual@mutualpublishing.com
www.mutualpublishing.com

Printed in Korea

Table of Contents

Preserves, Dressings and Condiments

Beverages

Glossary

Introduction

Mangoes and papayas are perhaps the only fruits in Hawai'i that are used as gauges for the time of year and the economy. "Mango season" in a Hawai'i resident's mind is of importance whether or not one has a mango tree—it means warmer weather, lots of cleaning up to do from fallen mangoes and flowers and, hopefully, plenty of luscious mangoes to give to or receive from friends and family. The most common residential fruit tree, it takes little effort to find someone who has one in his or her backyard. No matter how many mangoes are eaten through the season, they are always welcome at the table.

Fewer people grow papayas, but everyone loves them and they are a breakfast staple. The price of papayas is always a popular topic, and one way to get a local person's attention is to tell your favorite source of low cost, high quality papayas. But even when the price climbs over a dollar a pound for these mellow and sweet fruits, despite the gnashing of teeth, they're still inevitably bought.

Highly nutritious and delicious on its own, it's difficult to prepare a dish to improve on the plain mango or papaya's charms, but this is exactly what the recipes in this book have been chosen to do. This international selection of dishes offers a wide array of exciting flavors to enjoy. From the cool tangy Green Papaya Salad to the glorious Flambéed Mangoes, you'll love every bite.

MANGO BASICS—Mango Varieties

1. Indian vs. Philippine

There are two "races" of mangoes. The Indian mango is nearly round or plump oval in shape, is usually tinged with red and has a stronger, more complex flavor. Indian mangoes are the choicest for eating raw and include the most popular backyard varieties, Pirie (known as Paheri on the Mainland) and Haden. The Philippine mango is long and kidney-shaped and usually greenish. Some people enjoy eating the Philippine type raw when ripe, but the majority of Hawai'i residents use them under ripe for pickling and preserves.

2. Shopping for Mangoes

It can be a challenge to know exactly what variety of mango is being sold at a market, as they are often only labeled as "mangoes" with no other identification. Many of the mangoes sold for commercial consumption look the same, so if you want to know the variety you're buying, you'll need to check the box. The shipping crate of the mangoes will have the variety name printed on it. If the crate is not on display, you might want to ask the produce person to get the information for you.

Pirie (Paheri) mangoes are among the world's most exquisite, as they have a complex, spicy and musky flavor and no stringy fiber. When ripe, they are penetratingly sweet. Piries are somewhat heart-shaped and rounded, with an orange cast when ripe. They tend to be smaller than most other mangoes, about 3 to 4 inches at the widest point.

Haden mangoes have a simpler, more peach-like flavor than the Pirie, and have a slight amount of fiber near the stem. Because their flavor is straightforward, they are popular with people new to eating mangoes. Hadens can be larger than 6 inches at the widest point, and are oval in shape, with a bright red to purplish bloom.

Kent is a variety often found at supermarkets, and is similar in appearance but slightly more flavorful than the Haden.

Keitt is a variety that remains green even when ripe, so you will need to check for ripeness by feel. A slight softening (not mushiness or wetness) will indicate that the fruit will be sweet.

Judging the Mango from its Cover

The skin color of the mango is a good indicator of ripeness. A solid green usually indicates that the mango will be tart in flavor and the flesh will be quite hard. In some rare cases, the variety of mango will remain green even when ripe and you will need to judge the ripeness by feel (see Keitt mango, above).

An unripe mango will be very firm and will not yield to pressure from your fingers. Unripe mangoes are refreshing in their own right and can be used in salads raw as well as cooked or pickled in preserves.

Mangoes are also enjoyed half ripe, or nearly ripe, when the mango is half to three-quarters green and is beginning to soften. At this stage, the flavor is tart-sweet, and has the greatest complexity. Most recipes in this book are designed for mangoes that are in this stage of ripeness.

A fully ripe mango will only have the slightest hint of green, and will be yellow, orange and/or red according to variety. Ripe mangoes can be extremely sweet with only a hint of acid.

Don't be Rash

One of the most exciting taste treats in Hawai'i is a freshly picked mango. If you are going to do your own picking, please be aware that a large number of people are allergic to mango sap. The sticky sap will run copiously out of the stem ends of mangoes and can cause an extremely itchy rash. Avoid touching the sap, or, if your skin is very sensitive wear gloves. You might consider wearing rubber gloves while peeling mangoes, too. The peeled flesh of the mango will be free of this allergen.

PAPAYA BASICS—Papaya Varieties

The papaya has two distinct types: Hawaiian and Mexican. The Hawaiian varieties are what you find in supermarkets. Many are of the Solo variety—a type brought to Hawai'i from Barbados in 1911. The current popular varieties are strains of the Solo such as Kamiya and Sunrise. The most recent hybrid from the University of Hawai'i is the Rainbow papaya, a richly flavored Solo type with genetically engineered disease resistance to ringspot virus. All Hawaiian papayas turn yellow when ripe, and have flesh that ranges from the Kamiya's medium yellow to reddish orange in the Sunrise variety. The flesh is mellow, slightly musky and sweet when ripe, bland when under-ripe.

The Mexican papaya is less frequently seen in Hawai'i. It is a much larger papaya that may weigh up to 10 pounds and be more than 15 inches long. When ripe, these papayas have a less intense flavor than the Hawaiian varieties, and are less sweet. This type of papaya has firm flesh which is crunchy and somewhat like cucumber. It is best eaten green in Thai and Vietnamese salads. These papayas can be found in Chinatown or in Southeast Asian markets.

Selecting Papayas

Choose Hawaiian papayas that are yellowish when buying, as solid green papayas never ripen properly after they've been picked, even if they turn yellow on the outside. Make sure they are free from soft spots and the skin is smooth and unwrinkled.

SALADS

Chinese Duck and Mango Salad

Serves 4 to 6

*Many Chinese restaurants sell roast ducks
to take home. Chinese grocery stores and take-out
shops are also good sources.*

Vinaigrette
1 tablespoon red wine vinegar
1 tablespoon toasted white sesame seeds
2 tablespoons extra virgin olive oil
2 teaspoons sesame oil
1 teaspoon hot sauce

1 Chinese roast duck
1 red bell pepper, cut into thin slices
1 small sweet onion (Vidalia or Maui), sliced thin
1 medium mango, peeled and seeded
1 medium head radicchio
1 medium head Mānoa or Boston lettuce
1 medium head romaine lettuce
1/4 cup chopped roasted peanuts
1/2 cup kim chee, chopped
1/4 cup shredded carrot
3 teaspoons chopped fresh cilantro (Chinese parsley)
5 mint leaves, sliced thin

Combine vinaigrette ingredients in a small mixing bowl and set aside at room temperature.

Remove meat from the duck, and tear or cut duck meat into bite-size pieces.

continued on next page

Cut mango into 1/2-inch pieces. Place mango pieces in large salad bowl with red pepper and onion. Tear the radicchio and lettuces into bite-size pieces and add to bowl. Add the peanuts, kim chee and carrots, and toss. Keep chilled.

If duck is cold, gently warm before serving so duck is room temperature to lukewarm. Pour dressing over greens, and mix well. Serve greens, place duck meat over greens and garnish with coriander and mint.

Curried Chicken and Mango Salad with Cashews

Serves 6

4 cups diced cooked chicken
4 tablespoons fresh lemon juice
2 ripe mangoes, peeled, seeded and cut into 3/4-inch pieces
1 cup chopped celery
4 green onions, chopped
1/4 cup plain yogurt
1/4 cup mayonnaise
1-1/2 teaspoons curry powder
1/2 teaspoon ground cumin
Salt and pepper to taste
1 cup chopped roasted cashews
2 tablespoons chopped fresh cilantro (Chinese parsley), if desired

In a large bowl, toss together chicken, lemon juice and mangoes. Add celery and green onions. In a small bowl whisk together yogurt, mayonnaise, curry and cumin. Add dressing to chicken mixture and combine well. Taste, and add salt and pepper as needed.

Just before serving, garnish with cashews and coriander (if desired).

Green Papaya Salad

*See Introduction for pointers
on selecting papayas to be eaten raw.*

1/2 pound green papaya
1 clove garlic
2 or 3 red chili peppers, seeded (optional)
1 tomato, sliced in strips
1 to 2 tablespoons fish sauce
3 tablespoons lime juice
1 tablespoon sugar
1 tablespoon chopped roasted peanuts
Lettuce leaves or cabbage leaves trimmed to 4-inch squares
Mint leaves
Lime wedges

Peel and seed papaya, shred into long, thin strips. Place in a bowl of ice water to crisp. Drain thoroughly.

Grind together garlic and chili peppers in a food processor or mortar. Mix together the papaya, tomato, fish sauce, sugar and lime juice; add in garlic paste and toss lightly. Sprinkle with chopped peanuts.

Serve with lettuce or cabbage leaves, mint and lime wedges.

How to Eat:
Place a portion of papaya salad on a lettuce or cabbage leaf, add a mint leaf and form a packet to eat with the fingers.

Balsamic Papaya Salad

Serves 4

2 teaspoons balsamic vinegar
2 teaspoons fresh lemon juice
1/2 teaspoon salt
1/4 teaspoon black pepper
3 tablespoons extra virgin olive oil
1 (1-pound) firm ripe papaya, peeled, seeded and cut into
    1/2-inch cubes
1 large tomato, cut into 1/2-inch cubes
1 small red onion, halved and thinly sliced
1/3 cup fresh basil leaves, thinly sliced

Whisk together vinegar, lemon juice, salt and pepper; then add oil, whisking until emulsified. Add remaining ingredients and toss until coated.

Chilled Mango and Cucumber Soup

Makes about 6 cups

2 mangoes (2 pounds total), peeled and pitted
2 cucumbers (1-1/2 pounds total)
3 tablespoons finely chopped red onion
3 tablespoons fresh lime juice, or to taste
2 tablespoons chopped fresh cilantro (Chinese parsley)
1 teaspoon salt

Finely chop 1 mango and 1 cucumber and set aside. Coarsely chop remaining mango and cucumber and puree with 1/4 cup water in a blender until almost smooth. Transfer to a bowl and stir in finely chopped mango and cucumber, onion, lime juice and 1 cup cold water. Place bowl in larger bowl of ice and cold water and stir until cool.

Just before serving, stir in cilantro and salt.

Papayas with Crabmeat Salad

Serves 4

6-1/2 ounces canned or cooked fresh crabmeat, flaked
1/2 cup thinly sliced celery
1 lime
1/2 cup toasted slivered almonds
2 ripe papayas, halved and seeded

Mix crabmeat, celery and juice from half of the lime. Add almonds, mix salad and stuff into papaya halves. Garnish with wedges cut from remaining half of lime.

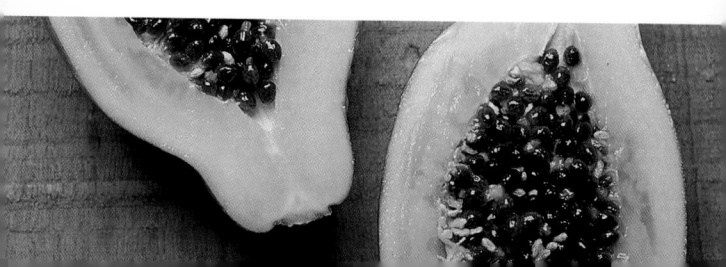

Turkey Mango Salad

Serves 6

Dressing
1/2 teaspoon lime zest
1/4 cup lime juice
2 tablespoons vegetable oil
1 tablespoon honey
1-1/2 teaspoons grated ginger
1/2 teaspoon salt
1/8 teaspoon ground red pepper

3 cups diced roast turkey
1 mango, peeled, seeded and diced
1 cup hulled and quartered strawberries
2 scallions, sliced diagonally
2 cups bite-size spinach leaves
2 cups bite-size lettuce leaves

Whisk dressing ingredients in a large bowl until blended.

Add turkey, mango, strawberries and scallions. Stir to coat.
Add greens and toss to mix. Serve immediately after mixing.

Papayas with Shrimp Salad

Serves 4

1-1/2 cups cooked shrimp, shelled, deveined and cut into chunks
1/2 cup mayonnaise
1 tablespoon lemon juice
1 tablespoon minced onion
Salt and pepper to taste
2 ripe papayas
Lime wedges

Mix shrimp, mayonnaise, lemon juice and onion and season to taste. (Lots of freshly ground pepper is delicious in this dish.)

Cut papayas in half and remove seeds. Stuff papaya halves with shrimp salad and garnish with lime wedges.

Avocado and
Papaya Salad

Serves 4

3 tablespoons fresh lime juice
1 tablespoon olive oil
Salt and pepper to taste
2 ripe papayas
2 red or pink grapefruits
1 medium ripe avocado
1 small head red leaf lettuce, washed and dried
1/4 cup minced onion

In a small bowl, whisk together lime juice and oil. Season with salt and pepper. Cut papaya lengthwise and remove skin. Scoop out and discard seeds. Slice thinly. With paring knife, remove skin and white pith from grapefruit. Working over a bowl to catch juice, cut sections from the membrane. Halve, peel, pit and thinly slice avocado. Line a large platter with lettuce leaves and arrange papaya, grapefruit sections and avocado slices on top. Add grapefruit juice to dressing and drizzle over salad. Sprinkle with onion and serve immediately.

Spicy Mango Salad

Serves 6

1 ripe mango
1 green mango
2 habanero (very hot) or 4 Serrano (mildly hot) chilies, seeded
    and minced
2 shallots, finely chopped
1/2 cup cilantro (Chinese parsley), chopped
1 tablespoon Thai fish sauce
Juice from 1 lime
2 teaspoons granulated sugar
1 pinch salt

Peel mangoes and cut flesh into thin slices. Place mango slices in bowl and add remaining ingredients. Mix thoroughly.

ENTRÉES

Broiled Chicken Thighs
with Mango Sauce

Serves 4

1 small mango, peeled and pitted
1 tablespoon plus 2 teaspoons vegetable oil
1 jalapeño chili, seeded and minced (optional)
1/3 cup thinly sliced fresh basil leaves
3/4 cup canned low-salt chicken broth
1-1/2 tablespoons brown sugar
1 tablespoon soy sauce
Salt and pepper to taste
8 chicken thighs

Puree mango in food processor. Set aside 1/2 cup puree
(reserve any remaining puree for another use).

Heat 1 tablespoon oil in medium skillet over medium heat.
Add garlic and jalapeño, then basil; sauté just until basil wilts,
about 1 minute. Add broth, brown sugar and soy sauce. Bring
to boil, stirring occasionally. Reduce heat to low and simmer
3 minutes. Gradually whisk in mango puree. Simmer until
sauce thickens and coats spoon, about 5 minutes. Season to
taste with salt and pepper.

Prepare the grill or preheat broiler. Brush chicken with 2 teaspoons oil. Sprinkle with salt and pepper. Grill or broil chicken
until cooked through. Transfer to plates.

Rewarm sauce over low heat, stirring occasionally. Drizzle
over chicken.

Grilled 'Ahi with Papaya-Basil Sauce

Serves 4

1 cup olive oil
5 sprigs fresh basil
Salt and white pepper to taste
4 (7-ounce) 'ahi steaks
1 ripe, firm medium papaya
3 shallots, peeled and sliced thinly
3 button mushrooms, sliced
1 cup dry white wine
1/2 cup heavy cream
4 tablespoons (1/2 stick) cold unsalted butter, in pieces

Prepare the grill. (If using oven broiler instead, fish may be placed on broiling pan.)

In a shallow pan, combine olive oil, two sprigs of basil, salt and pepper and add fish steaks. Marinate at least 15 minutes.

Peel the papaya and discard the seeds. Cut flesh into small chunks. In a nonreactive (glass, enamel or nonstick) saucepan, combine the shallots, mushrooms, wine and papaya. Over medium heat, reduce the wine by two-thirds, and then add the cream. Reduce by two-thirds again and whisk in the butter, one piece at a time, until the sauce thickens slightly. Pour the mixture into a blender, and add the remaining basil and blend until smooth. Adjust the seasoning if necessary.

Grill the fish (or broil) for about 2 minutes on each side, and serve with the sauce. Do not cook fish past pink stage, as it will become dry.

Mango Chutney Spareribs

Serves 4

2 racks pork spareribs (about 6-1/2 pounds)

Sauce
1/4 cup dry sherry
1/2 cup soy sauce
1/2 cup mango chutney (store-bought or see recipe, p. 66),
    puréed
1/2 cup sugar
2 green onions, finely chopped
1 tablespoon finely chopped fresh ginger
2 large garlic cloves, minced

Preheat oven to 325 degrees.

Cut between bones to separate ribs. Boil ribs in water in large pot for about 15 minutes and drain off all water and fat. Combine sauce ingredients and blanched ribs in large Dutch oven and bake for 45 minutes.

Grilled Pork Tacos with Papaya Salsa

Serves 5

1/2 pound boneless pork, cut in 2 x 1/4-inch strips
Salt and pepper to taste
1/2 cup peeled, seeded and chopped papaya
1/2 cup chopped fresh pineapple
10 (6 to 7-inch diameter) flour tortillas, warmed
1-1/2 cups shredded Monterey Jack cheese
2 tablespoons butter, melted

Cook pork in 10-inch skillet over medium heat about 10 minutes, stirring occasionally, until no longer pink. Drain and season pork with salt and pepper. Stir in papaya and pineapple. Warm over medium heat, stirring occasionally, until heated through.

Heat oven to 425 degrees. Spoon about 1/4 cup of the pork mixture onto each tortilla and top each with about 2 tablespoons of cheese. Fold tortillas around filling. Arrange filled tortillas in ungreased jelly roll pan and brush with melted butter. Bake uncovered or until light golden brown. Serve with Papaya Salsa.

continued on next page

Papaya Salsa

1 ripe papaya, peeled, seeded and cut into 1/2-inch cubes
1 small red chili, seeded and finely minced
1/2 cup minced red onion
1/2 cup minced red bell pepper
1/2 cup chopped mint leaves
2 tablespoons lime juice

Mix ingredients, cover and refrigerate at least 30 minutes or until chilled.

Salmon in Papaya Red Thai Curry Sauce

Serves 4

Papaya Red Thai Curry Sauce

2 tablespoons sesame oil
2 ounces red Thai curry paste
2 shallots, peeled and finely minced
1 (1-inch) piece ginger, peeled and finely grated
4 cloves garlic, peeled and finely crushed
3 whole star anise pods
1 teaspoon toasted, cracked coriander seeds
1 cup rice vinegar
1 (14-ounce) can coconut milk
1 ripe papaya, peeled, seeded and roughly chopped

Place a 1-quart capacity saucepan over medium heat. Add the sesame oil, then the red Thai curry paste. Cook the paste for 2 minutes while gently stirring. Add shallots, ginger, garlic, star anise and coriander seeds. Stir these ingredients for 1 minute. Add vinegar and cook until reduced by half the original volume. Add coconut milk and papaya and simmer for 10 minutes on low heat. Puree in a blender until smooth. (Pulse the blender before running it so hot liquid doesn't expand and spatter.) Strain sauce and discard remaining pulp.

continued on next page

Caramelized Salmon

4 (8-ounce) salmon fillets, bones and skin removed
2/3 cup sugar
1/3 cup salt
2 tablespoons cracked black peppercorns
2 tablespoons cracked pink peppercorns
2 tablespoons toasted cracked coriander seeds
2 tablespoons vegetable oil

Preheat oven to 375 degrees. Mix together the sugar and spices. Place mixture in a shallow pie pan or plate. Press salmon fillets in the spice mixture on both sides. Bring a skillet to high heat. Add vegetable oil, and when hot, add salmon fillets. When amber caramel starts to form after about 1 minute, turn fillets over carefully. Place fillets in oven and bake for 4 minutes, or until medium rare.

To serve: Pool curry sauce on dishes and place salmon fillet over sauce.

DESSERTS

Sam Choy's Mango Bread

Makes two 9 x 5-inch loaves

Chef, cookbook author and TV celebrity Sam Choy is acknowledged as one of the foremost authorities of Hawaiian cuisine.

2 cups all-purpose flour
2 teaspoons baking soda
1 teaspoon baking powder
2 teaspoons cinnamon
3 eggs, well beaten
3/4 cup canola oil
1-1/2 cups granulated sugar
2 cups peeled and diced fresh mango
1/2 cup raisins
1/2 cup chopped macadamia nuts or walnuts
1/2 cup grated coconut

Preheat the oven to 350 degrees. Grease and flour two
9 x 5-inch loaf pans.

Sift the flour, baking soda, baking powder and cinnamon
together into a small bowl.

In a large mixing bowl, combine the eggs, oil and sugar. Add
dry ingredients and blend well. Fold in the mango, raisins,
nuts and coconut.

Pour batter into the loaf pans and bake for 45 to 60 minutes, or
until the bread is golden brown and a toothpick inserted in the
center of the loaf comes out clean. Let loaves cool in the pan for
10 to 15 minutes; then unmold and let cool completely on racks.

Papaya Cake with Liliko'i Frosting

Cake
1/2 cup (1 stick) butter, softened
1 cup granulated sugar
2 eggs, beaten
1 cup mashed papaya
2 cups sifted all-purpose flour
1/2 teaspoon cinnamon
1/2 teaspoon salt
3/4 teaspoon baking powder
1 teaspoon baking soda
1/2 teaspoon ground allspice
1/2 teaspoon ground cloves

Garnish
1/2 cup chopped macadamia nuts
1/2 cup coconut

Preheat the oven to 350 degrees. Grease and flour a 13 x 9-inch baking pan.

Cream the butter and sugar together until fluffy. Gradually add the beaten eggs and mashed papaya. Sift all the dry ingredients together and stir into the creamed butter mixture.

Pour into the prepared pan and bake for 25 minutes, or until a toothpick inserted in the center comes out clean. Cool in the pan. Ice with Lilikoʻi Frosting and sprinkle with chopped macadamia nuts and coconut.

Lilikoʻi Frosting
3 tablespoons butter
1-3/4 cups powdered sugar
3 tablespoons thawed frozen passion fruit juice concentrate

Cream butter. Add sugar gradually and cream until fluffy. Add passion fruit juice concentrate, beating until the icing is smooth and stiff enough to spread on the cake.

Mango Cream Cheese Pie

Makes one 9 x 13-inch pie, serves 12 to 16

Crust
2 cups sifted flour
1/2 cup powdered sugar, sifted
3/4 cup butter

Preheat oven to 350 degrees. Combine flour and powdered sugar and cut in butter until crumbs are the size of small peas. Press into bottom of 9 x 13-inch pan. Bake for 20 to 25 minutes or until light brown. Cool.

Cream Cheese Layer
8 ounces cream cheese
1/2 cup granulated sugar
1 teaspoon vanilla
1/2 cup whipping cream
1 tablespoon sugar

Beat cream cheese and 1/2 cup sugar until light and fluffy. Set aside. Beat whipping cream with 1 tablespoon sugar and vanilla until stiff. Fold into cream cheese mixture. Spread over cooled crust and chill until firm.

Mango Topping

2 envelopes unflavored gelatin
1 cup cold water
1 cup boiling water
1 cup granulated sugar (or less if mangoes are very ripe)
5 cups mangoes, peeled, diced and drained

Sprinkle gelatin over cold water to soften. Add boiling water and sugar and mix well. Let cool. Stir in mangoes and chill mixture until slightly thickened. Pour over cream cheese layer and chill until firm.

Tahitian Baked Papayas

Serves 6

3 ripe but firm papayas
6 small pieces vanilla bean
6 teaspoons butter
12 teaspoons brown sugar

Preheat oven to 350 degrees.

Peel the papayas and split each in half. Remove the seeds.

Arrange the papaya halves, cut side up, in a baking dish with about 1/2 inch of water over the bottom. Dot the center of each papaya half with a small piece of vanilla bean, a teaspoon of butter and two teaspoons of brown sugar. Bake until thoroughly tender, 45 minutes to 1 hour.

Mango Crisp

4 medium mangoes, peeled and thinly sliced
1/2 cup granulated sugar (use less with riper mangoes)
3/4 cup quick-cooking rolled oats (not instant or old-fashioned)
3/4 cup brown sugar
1/2 cup flour
1 teaspoon cinnamon
1/2 cup (1 stick) butter

Preheat oven to 350 degrees.

Toss mangoes with granulated sugar. Place mangoes in a greased 8-inch round pan.

Combine oats, brown sugar, flour and cinnamon. Cut in butter until mixture is crumbly. Sprinkle oat mixture evenly over mangoes.

Bake for 35 to 40 minutes or until top crust is browned and crisp.

Serve warm with ice cream or whipped cream.

Mango Upside-down Cake

Serves 8 to 10

1-1/2 cups all-purpose flour
1 teaspoon baking powder
1/4 teaspoon salt
1/2 cup (1 stick) unsalted butter, softened
1 cup granulated sugar
3 large eggs, 2 of them separated
1 teaspoon vanilla
1/2 cup mango nectar

Mango topping
2 (1-pound) firm-ripe mangoes, peeled
1/4 cup (1/2 stick) unsalted butter
1/2 cup packed brown sugar

Make topping: Cut mangoes into 3/8-inch thick slices. Melt butter in a small saucepan over moderate heat, then stir in brown sugar. Simmer, stirring, until butter is incorporated, 1 or 2 minutes. Spread mixture in bottom of a buttered 9 x 2-inch round baking pan and arrange mango slices on top, overlapping slices decoratively.

Make batter: Preheat oven to 350 degrees. Whisk together flour baking powder and salt. Beat together butter and sugar in a large bowl with an electric mixer at high speed until light and fluffy, about 6 minutes. Add whole egg and yolks one at a time, beating well after each addition. Beat in vanilla. Add half of flour mixture and mix at low speed until just combined. Mix in mango nectar, then add remaining flour mixture, mixing until just combined.

Beat egg whites in another bowl with cleaned beaters until they just hold stiff peaks, then fold into batter gently but thoroughly.

Gently spoon batter over mango topping and spread evenly. Bake in middle of oven until golden brown and a toothpick inserted in the center comes out clean, 55 to 60 minutes. Cool cake in pan on a rack 10 minutes. Run a thin knife around inside edge of pan, then invert a plate over pan and invert cake onto plate. Cool completely on plate on rack.

Serve cake at room temperature.

Double-crusted Mango Pie

Makes one 9-inch pie

Pastry
2 cups all-purpose flour
1 teaspoon salt
2/3 cup shortening
4 to 5 tablespoons cold water

Measure flour and salt into a bowl. Cut in shortening thoroughly. Sprinkle in water, a tablespoon at a time, mixing until all flour is moistened and dough almost cleans sides of bowl.

Divide dough in half and shape into two flattened rounds. With floured rolling pin, roll one round of dough 2 inches larger than pie pan. Use rolling pin to lift dough and ease into pie pan. Trim overhanging edge of pastry 1/2 inch from edge of pan. Keep dough-lined pie pan and remaining round cool.

Preheat oven to 425° degrees.

Pie Filling

4 cups ripe firm mango slices
1 cup granulated sugar
1/2 teaspoon cinnamon
1/4 teaspoon nutmeg
3 tablespoons cornstarch
1 tablespoon fresh orange juice
1 tablespoon butter

Mix sugar, spices and cornstarch together. Alternate layers of mango slices and sugar mixture in dough-lined pie pan. Sprinkle with orange juice and dot with butter.

Roll out second round of dough and cover pie. Trim overhanging edge 1 inch from rim of pan, seal with bottom crust and flute. Cut vents on top. Bake pie for 15 minutes, then reduce temperature to 350 degrees and continue baking for 30 minutes. Cool pie on rack before serving.

Mango Mousse Cake

Serves 8 to 10

Cake

1/2 cup sifted cake flour
1/2 teaspoon baking powder
2 large eggs
2 large egg yolks
1/2 cup sugar
2 tablespoons (1/4 stick) unsalted butter, melted

Position rack in center of oven and preheat to 400 degrees. Butter two 9-inch diameter cake pans with 1-1/2-inch-high sides. Line bottom of pans with waxed paper. Butter paper and dust lightly with flour.

Sift flour and baking powder into medium bowl. Using electric mixer, beat eggs and yolks in large bowl until frothy. Gradually add 1/2 cup sugar and beat until pale yellow and slowly dissolving ribbon forms when beaters are lifted, about 4 minutes. Fold in flour mixture. Fold in 1 heaping tablespoon batter into melted butter. Fold butter mixture back into batter. Divide batter between pans. Bake until cakes are golden brown around edges and toothpick inserted into centers comes out clean, about 10 minutes. Cool completely in pans on rack.

Mango Mousse

1/4 cup orange liqueur
1 packet unflavored gelatin
2-1/2 pounds ripe mangoes, peeled, pitted and chopped
1/2 cup sugar
1 cup whipped cream

continued on next page

Pour liqueur into small bowl; sprinkle gelatin over. Let gelatin soften 10 minutes. Puree mangoes in processor. Measure puree and return 2-1/2 cups to work bowl of processor (reserve remainder for garnish). Add sugar to mango puree in processor and blend well. Set bowl of gelatin in saucepan of simmering water. Stir until gelatin dissolves. Add gelatin mixture to mango in processor and blend. Whip cream in large bowl to soft peaks. Fold in mango mixture.

Transfer one cake layer to 9-inch springform pan with 2-3/4-inch-high sides. Spread mango mousse over cake. Place second layer on top of mousse. Press lightly. Wrap tightly with plastic and refrigerate at least 4 hours. (Can be prepared one day ahead.)

Frosting

1 cup chilled whipping cream
1 tablespoon powdered sugar
1-1/2 teaspoons orange liqueur

1-1/2 cups toasted sweetened coconut
1 ripe mango, peeled pitted and sliced

Whip cream until soft peaks form. Add sugar and liqueur and beat until firm peaks form.

Release springform pan sides. Transfer cake to platter. Frost top and sides of cake with whipped cream frosting. Press toasted coconut on sides. Garnish top with mango slices. Brush mango with reserved puree.

Fresh Papaya Pie

Makes one 8-inch pie

Pastry
2 cups all-purpose flour
1 teaspoon salt
2/3 cup shortening
4 to 5 tablespoons cold water

Measure flour and salt into bowl. Cut in shortening thoroughly. Sprinkle in water, a tablespoon at a time, mixing until all flour is moistened and dough almost cleans sides of bowl.

Divide dough in half and shape into two flattened rounds. With floured rolling pin, roll one round of dough 2 inches larger than pie pan. Use rolling pin to lift dough and ease into pie pan. Trim overhanging edge of pastry 1/2 inch from rim of pan. Keep dough-lined pie pan and remaining dough round cool.

Preheat oven to 350 degrees.

Filling
1/2 cup unsweetened pineapple juice
3/4 cup granulated sugar
3 to 4 cups papaya, peeled, seeded and sliced
1 tablespoon cornstarch
2 tablespoons water

continued on next page

Boil pineapple juice with sugar. Add sliced papaya and cook for 15 minutes. Remove papaya from liquid. Mix cornstarch with water, add to juice, and cook until thickened to desired consistency, stirring constantly.

Fill crust with papaya, then pour pineapple juice mixture over fruit.

Roll out second round of dough and cover pie. Trim overhanging edge 1 inch from rim of pan, seal with bottom crust and flute edge decoratively. Cut vents on top. Bake pie for 1 hour.

Mango Cobbler

Serves 4 to 6

2 mangoes, peeled, seeded and sliced
2 tablespoons lime juice
1/2 teaspoon ground nutmeg
1 cup all-purpose flour
2 teaspoons baking powder
1/4 teaspoon salt
1/2 cup brown sugar
3 tablespoons butter, softened
1/2 cup milk

Preheat oven to 375 degrees.

Combine mangoes, lime juice and nutmeg in mixing bowl.
Spoon fruit into lightly greased 8-inch square baking pan.

Combine flour, baking powder, salt and brown sugar in mixing
bowl. With pastry cutter, cut margarine into flour until mixture
resembles coarse meal. Stir in milk; blend batter until
smooth. Spread batter evenly over fruit. Bake cobbler for 20 to
25 minutes.

Serve warm with yogurt, ice cream or whipped cream.

Papaya or Mango Sorbet

Makes 6 cups

4 ripe mangoes or 3 ripe papayas (3-1/2 pounds total)
1 cup Simple Syrup (see recipe below)
3 tablespoons fresh lime juice, or to taste

Wash and dry fruit. Peel, seed and cut fruit coarsely. Place fruit in blender, add syrup and lime juice and puree until smooth.

Freeze fruit puree in an ice cream maker, and follow manufacturer's instructions.

Simple Syrup
3 cups sugar
3 cups water

In a saucepan bring sugar and water to a boil, stirring constantly, and boil until sugar is completely dissolved. Cool syrup. Syrup may be made ahead and chilled, covered. This syrup will keep at least 2 months in the refrigerator.

Makes 4-1/2 cups syrup.

Thai Sticky Rice with Mango

Serves 6

1-1/2 cups glutinous (sweet) rice
1-1/3 cups well-stirred canned unsweetened coconut milk
1/3 cup plus 3 tablespoons granulated sugar
1/4 teaspoon salt
1 large mango, peeled, seeded and sliced thickly

In the bowl of your rice cooker wash rice well in several changes of cold water until water is clear. Soak rice in hot water to cover for 1 hour.

Meanwhile, bring 1 cup coconut milk, 1/3 cup sugar and salt to a boil in a small saucepan. Stir until sugar is dissolved, and remove from heat.

Drain rice well in a sieve. Discard soaking water. Transfer rice back into empty rice cooker bowl, and add coconut milk mixture and enough water to reach 1/2 inch above rice. Cook rice and let stand 15 minutes to steam.

In cleaned small saucepan, slowly boil remaining 1/3 cup coconut milk with remaining 3 tablespoons sugar, stirring occasionally, 1 minute. Cool, then chill until thickened slightly.

To serve, mold 1/4 cup servings of rice on dessert plates. Drizzle desserts with sauce and divide mango slices among plates.

Flambéed Mangoes

2 small or 1 large mango (about 1 pound), peeled, seeded and sliced
1-1/2 tablespoons unsalted butter
1-1/2 tablespoons granulated sugar
Zest of 1/2 orange
Zest of 1/2 lime
1 ounce Triple Sec or Cointreau
Juice of 1/2 orange
Juice of 1/2 lime
1 ounce white tequila
Sorbet or Ice Cream (optional)

Have all the ingredients for this dish set out in decorative dishes near chafing dish. (This is a pyrotechnics show, after all.) Gather the audience.

Melt the butter in a chafing dish, stir in the sugar and continue stirring until it has dissolved. Add the citrus zest and liqueur, heat the mixture, and flame it.

When flames have died down, add the orange and lime juices and cook until reduced, about 2 minutes. Add the mango slices and heat until the syrup begins to bubble.

Add the tequila, heat through, and flame again. Serve immediately, by itself, or over sorbet or ice cream.

Mango Cheesecake

Serves 8

Crust
1-1/2 cups crushed graham crackers
1/2 cup desiccated coconut (available at health food stores)
1-1/2 teaspoons cinnamon
2-1/2 tablespoons granulated sugar
2/3 cup melted butter

Mix the crust ingredients and press into bottom of 9-inch springform pan and chill until ready to use.

Filling
2-1/2 tablespoons unflavored gelatin
1-1/4 tablespoons lemon zest
2 tablespoons lemon juice
1/2 cup boiling water
1/2 cup granulated sugar
3 egg yolks
12 ounces cream cheese, softened
1 pound mashed mango pulp
1/2 cup cold water
1-1/2 cups sour cream
2/3 cup whipping cream

continued on next page

Put the gelatin, lemon zest, lemon juice and boiling water in a blender and whirl for about 30 seconds. Add sugar, yolks and cream cheese. Whirl on high speed for another 30 seconds. Reserve 1/2 cup of mango pulp. Add remainder to blender with cold water and sour cream. Blend until well combined. Pour filling into prepared crust and chill until firm.

Whip the cream and fold in reserved mango pulp. Spread evenly over top of cheesecake and serve.

Phyllo Mango Triangles

Makes 20 triangles

4 cups sliced mangoes
3/4 cup granulated sugar (less for riper mangoes)
1/3 cup water
1 teaspoon lemon juice
1 teaspoon cinnamon
1/8 teaspoon freshly ground nutmeg
1 tablespoon tapioca
3 tablespoons cornstarch
3 tablespoons water
1/2 cup (1 stick) butter, melted
1 box phyllo pastry
Powdered sugar

Cook the first seven ingredients over medium high heat, stirring occasionally until it starts to boil. Mix cornstarch and water together, add to mango mixture and stir well, cooking until thickened. Let cool.

Preheat oven to 350 degrees.

Follow defrosting instructions on phyllo box. Unroll phyllo. With long side facing you, cut phyllo into four strips approximately 4 x 12 inches in size. (Kitchen shears are very helpful for this task.) Use caution, as phyllo is very thin and fragile.

continued on next page

Brush a 4 x 12-inch sheet with butter, top with another sheet, and continue to butter and stack until you have three layers. Butter the top sheet too. Place a heaping tablespoon of mango filling in one corner of the pastry. Fold into a triangle (like folding a flag) and place on greased cookie sheet. Repeat procedure with the rest of the pastry and filling. Bake for 15 to 20 minutes. Dust with powdered sugar.

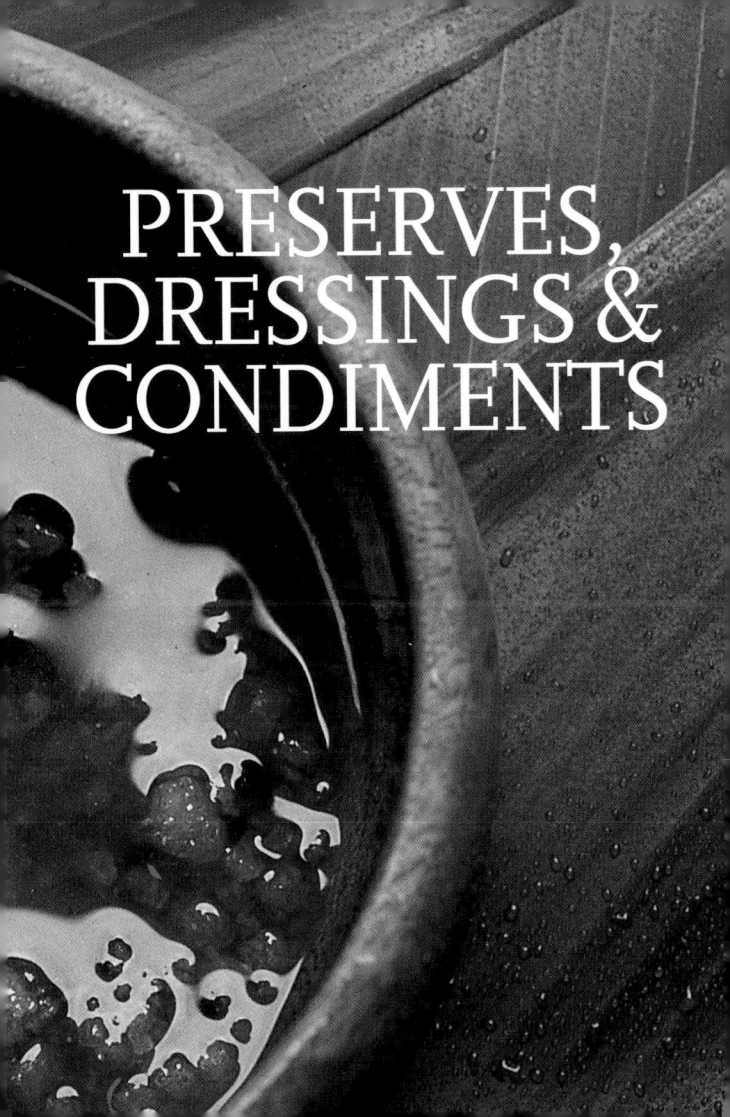

PRESERVES, DRESSINGS & CONDIMENTS

Kusuma Cooray's Mango Chutney

Makes 2 quarts

*A highly respected chef-instructor at
Hawai'i's Culinary Institute of the Pacific
and the former executive chef at The Willows,
Kusuma Cooray popularized the cuisine
of her home country Sri Lanka.
This is her family's mango chutney recipe.*

2 packed quarts half-ripe mango, peeled, seeded and sliced
   into 1/4 by 2-inch pieces
1 cup dark seedless raisins
4 cups granulated sugar
4 cups cider vinegar
1 yellow onion, minced
4 tablespoons minced ginger
4 tablespoons minced garlic
2 teaspoons crushed red pepper flakes
1 teaspoon freshly grated nutmeg
1 teaspoon ground cloves
2-inch piece of cinnamon stick
6 cardamoms pods
Salt to taste

Wipe mangoes, drying off all moisture. Set aside with raisins.

Place remaining ingredients in a nonreactive pan and simmer over low heat for 15 minutes. Add mangoes and raisins. Simmer until mangoes turn transparent and chutney is thick, about 2 to 2-1/2 hours.

Let chutney cool, ladle into sterilized jars, cover and refrigerate. Chutney keeps up to 3 months.

Pickled Mango

Makes 4 quarts

16 cups (4 quarts) peeled green mango chunks
3 cups water
2 cups cider vinegar
2-1/2 cups brown sugar
1/4 cup Hawaiian or other sea salt
1 tablespoon Chinese five spice
1/3 pound seedless li hing mui (salty preserved plums)
1 teaspoon mace
2 tablespoons minced ginger

Place mango chunks into sterilized jars. Place remaining ingredients in large saucepan over medium heat. Bring to a boil and cook 5 minutes while stirring to dissolve brown sugar. Pour pickle syrup over mangoes and seal jars immediately. Cool to room temperature, then refrigerate.

Papaya Seed Dressing

Makes 2 cups

*The peppery taste of crushed papaya seeds adds texture
and piquant flavor to a vinegar and oil salad dressing.
Use this dressing on greens, fruit salad or as a marinade.
Papaya seeds may be crushed in a food processor
using a metal blade or in a blender.*

4 tablespoons crushed papaya seeds
2 tablespoons fresh rosemary or 2 teaspoons dried rosemary
1 tablespoon fresh tarragon or 1 teaspoon dried tarragon
1 garlic clove, minced
1 tablespoon lime zest, lemon zest or passion fruit pulp
1/3 cup red wine vinegar
2 cups salad oil, olive oil or macadamia nut oil

Place all ingredients except oil into a large mixing bowl and
stir to moisten. Use a wire whisk to combine the oil with the
dressing ingredients. Chill at least 1 hour before serving.

Spicy Mango Ketchup

Makes 1 quart

1 tablespoon butter
2 tablespoons chopped fresh garlic
1 cup red onion, chopped
1 mango, peeled, seeded and diced
3 cups rice vinegar
1 (20-ounce) bottle ketchup
1 pound box brown sugar
3 tablespoons pureed canned chipotle chilies
2 tablespoons ground ginger
1 tablespoon cinnamon
1-1/2 tablespoons ground cloves
Salt and pepper to taste

In a saucepan melt butter over medium heat, add garlic and onions and stir until translucent. Add the rest of the ingredients and bring to a boil. Reduce heat and simmer for 10 minutes. Season to taste with salt and pepper. Puree and store in refrigerator.

BEVERAGES

Papaya Berry Yogurt Shake

Serves 3

Banana and berries are a classic pairing in smoothies, but add papaya and your drink takes on tropical appeal.

1 cup berry yogurt
1 small banana
1 cup fresh or frozen berries (reserve 3 whole berries
    for garnish)
1 cup papaya, peeled, seeded and chopped
1/4 cup apple juice
2 tablespoons lemon juice
2 cups ice cubes
2 teaspoons granulated sugar (optional)

Combine yogurt, cut-up banana, berries, papaya, apple juice, and lemon juice in a blender; cover blender and pulse-blend about 15 seconds.

With blender running, gradually add ice cubes, blending until smooth.

Top off with a berry if desired. Serve immediately.

Orange-Mango Ice Cream Shake

Serves 2

The colors of the sky at dawn distinguish this creamy pick-me-up.

1 medium-size ripe mango*, peeled, seeded and chopped
1 cup orange juice
1/2 teaspoon vanilla extract
1 cup vanilla ice cream, softened
1 cup ice cubes

In a blender, combine all ingredients until smooth.

*Substitutions:
1 cup fresh strawberries for mango
Pineapple juice for orange juice
Pineapple sherbet for ice cream

Mango Daiquiri

Serves 2

2 ounces light rum
1 large ripe mango, peeled and seeded
1 tablespoon lemon juice
1 teaspoon sugar (optional)
Scoop of cracked ice

Combine rum, mango, lemon juice and sugar (if using) in a blender. Blend on high speed for 30 seconds. Gradually add cracked ice, blending until drink is of a slushy consistency.

Glossary

A

'Ahi:
Hawaiian name for yellowfin or bigeye tuna. Also called shibi in Japanese. When the term 'ahi is used, it is assumed that fresh tuna, rather than canned, is meant.

C

Cilantro:
leaves of the coriander plant. Also known as Chinese parsley.

Coconut:
the fruit of the coconut palm, consisting of a fibrous husk surrounding a large seed; the seed contains edible white flesh, which is often shredded and used in food and confections, and for oil.

Coconut milk:
the liquid extracted by squeezing the grated meat of a coconut; most often found in canned and frozen forms.

Cut in:
to mix a solid fat into flour and other dry ingredients by using a pair of knives or a pastry cutter to cut the fat into small pieces while mixing. This method produces small granules of fat mixed with the dry ingredients.

F

Fish sauce:
a thin, brown and salty liquid made from salted anchovies. Vietnam, Thailand and the Philippines produce this condiment, where it is used much like soy sauce is used in Japan or China.

Five spice powder :
a spice blend generally consisting of ground cloves, fennel seeds, star anise, cinnamon and Szechwan pepper; used in Chinese and Vietnamese cuisines.

G

Ginger:
the gnarled rhizome of a tall, flowering plant (*Zingiber officinale*) native to China. In Hawai'i, where it is grown, it is most frequently used fresh. Though also available powdered, pickled or candied, these forms are not good substitutes for fresh ginger.

Glutinous rice :
also called sticky rice or sweet rice. This type of rice has a high starch content, which causes the grains to stick together more than other varieties.

Green papaya:
> the unripe form of the papaya, usually shredded and used in salads and stir-fries in Southeast Asian cuisines.

H

Habanero:
> a tropical pepper having small, round, extremely hot green to red fruit that is often used in making sauces, salsa and spicy foods.

Hawaiian or sea salt:
> a coarse sea salt gathered in tidal pools after a storm or high tide. Hawaiians sometimes mix it with a red clay to make alae salt. Substitute kosher salt.

J

Jalapeño:
> a small- to medium-sized green chili pepper whose heat content ranges from mild to hot, depending on its cultivation; when there are no jalapeños on hand, Serrano peppers make a good substitute.

K

Kim chee:
> a very spicy Korean vegetable pickle—usually Chinese cabbage. The main seasonings are red chilies, garlic, ginger and green onions.

L

Li hing mui:
> salty-sweet dried plums, usually eaten as a candy. These are found in Chinese preserved fruit (crack seed) stores.

Liliko'i:
> the Hawaiian name for passion fruit, which is a small yellow, purple or brown oval fruit of the passion fruit vine. The flavor is delicate but somewhat sharp and perfume-like. Passion fruit is a natural substitute for lemon juice. Passion fruit concentrate can be found in the frozen juice section of many markets. Substitute oranges.

M

Mace:
> an aromatic spice made from the dried, waxy, scarlet or yellowish covering that partly encloses the kernel of the nutmeg.

Macadamia nuts:
> rich, slightly sweet nuts that are a major crop in Hawai'i; often called "Mac Nuts."

Mango:
> a sweet and aromatic fruit that ranges in size from 1/2 to 2 pounds and tastes like a slightly resinous peach. Varieties range in color from greenish yellow to red when ripe.

Mānoa lettuce:
> the most common type of lettuce grown in Hawai'i, formally known as green mignonette; it is favored for its small semi-head and the buttery flavor of its medium- to dark-green leaves.

Maui onion:
> large white onion noted for its sweet flavor, grown in Kula, the upcountry region of Maui. Substitute with other sweet onions, such as Vidalia.

N

Nonreactive:
> a term describing cooking or serving utensils made of materials that don't react with acids or brine to discolor foods or create toxic substances. Items made with undamaged nonstick surfaces, enamel, flameproof glass or stainless steel are non-reactive. Uncoated aluminum, iron or copper items are reactive.

P

Papaya:
> in Hawai'i this sweet, yellow, pear-shaped fruit is about 6 to 10 inches long. A common size will yield about 1-1/2 to 2 cups flesh.

Phyllo:
> pastry dough made from flour and water into very thin sheets. The sheets are layered with melted butter and fried or baked to make sweet or savory pastries. Found in the freezer section in supermarkets.

Pūpū:
> Hawaiian word meaning appetizer or snack to go with drinks.

R

Rice vinegar:
> a type of vinegar made from rice wine; generally clear with a pale straw color. Generally, rice vinegar is mellow and lower in acid than other vinegars.

S

Sesame oil:
> oil pressed from the sesame seed is available in two forms. Pressing the raw seed produces an oil which is light in color and flavor and can be used for a wide variety of purposes. When the oil is pressed from toasted sesame seeds, it is dark in color with a much stronger flavor. It is this darker version that is to be used in the recipes of this book.

Sesame seeds:
> the edible seeds of a plant of the Pedaliaceae family that have a distinctive nutty flavor. They come in black or white varieties, and are known as benne seeds and goma.

Shallot:
> this member of the onion family forms a bulb more like a garlic bulb and has a subtler flavor than green onions.

Soy sauce:
> a sauce made from fermented boiled soybeans and roasted wheat or barley; its color ranges from light or dark brown and its flavor is generally rich and salty. Used extensively in Chinese and Japanese cuisines as a flavoring, condiment and a cooking medium.

Star anise:
> the dried star-shaped fruit of the Chinese magnolia used for their strong licorice fragrance.

T

Thai curry paste:
> a paste of fresh herbs and spices used for making Thai curries. Yellow curry paste is most influenced by Indian cuisine—seasoned with turmeric, coriander and cinnamon—and is the mildest. Red curry paste is accented with lots of shallots and red chilies, and green is the most herbal and the hottest.

V

Vanilla:
> a flavoring extract prepared from the cured seedpods of any of various tropical American vines of the genus Vanilla in the orchid family. Vanilla flavoring is also synthetically produced, but natural flavoring from the vanilla bean is often favored.

Z

Zest:
> the colored portion of a citrus fruit's rind. When removing the zest from a citrus fruit, it's important to avoid removing the bitter white pith just below the colored portion.